TH DREAM TICKET

Henry Normal

INTRODUCTION (Second Edition)

This is the fourth in a series of books. Some of the pieces appeared in my 'Postcard from Crumpsall' column for CITY LIFE. A couple first appeared in the now defunct 'DO YOU BELIEVE IN CARPETWORLD'.

Additional pieces to first edition;

Life after forever
The dream of the Rood
Love poem to the reviewers
Southern Cemetry – The class of 92
Turning straight to the sports pages
A tribute to Michael Clarke
A tribute to L. S. Lowry
A tribute to Andy Warhol's wig
Middle age spread
Mid Wales crisis
The man who thought Craig Raine was responsible for the depletion of
     Scandinavian forests
My son the poet
Was Man an afterthought?
Is the universe God's bachelor pad?
Famous for a fifteenth of a second
Prayers for the imperfect
Sans pretension
Never play chess with an Anarcho-Nihilist
Mime doesn't pay

Pieces deleted;

Bike salesman to the aquatics
Short notice love poem
The ultimate in serious prose
A present from the Tower Ballroom
Please leave a dear John after the tone
Like ships that crash in the night

Pieces altered;

There will come a time . . .
Self mutilation . . .
Self Image being at the core of motivation
After all the rain that's fallen

DEDICATED TO JOHN BRAMWELL

All pieces by HENRY NORMAL.

Cover by EMMA DAMON.

PUBLISHED BY: A. K. PRESS
                   22 LUTTON PLACE
                   EDINBURGH
                   EH8 9PE

PRINTED IN GREAT BRITAIN BY UNICORN PRESS, SHEFFIELD.

CONTENTS

THE DREAM TICKET

THE FIRST FEW PAGES OF HER DIARY ARE ALWAYS WRITTEN NEAT

The first few pages of her diary are always written neat.
She is meticulous. First impressions last.

Around April she is no longer self conscious.
Her character busts the confines of set agenda.

Summer sees a casual familiarity. Some days she
Writes a rain storm. Some days life is too close to record.

September sees few notes but all highly personal.
Her comments becoming cryptic.

Somehow she never manages to finish a full year.
There is never a conclusion, or an acknowledgement to the
Nature of her final entry.
The last few pages of her diary are always blank.

For Christmas she will treat herself once more
And make a commitment once again.

THE FALL OF CONSUMER MAN

. . . and the next day the Lord God came forth into Eden and found a garden gnome.

Now this worried the Lord God for he knew he was infallible and he couldn't remember saying anything about let there be bad taste.

He called to Adam who was hiding behind a bush saying 'I want a word with you, about this craven image'. 'Frankly', sayeth the Lord, 'I'm disappointed, how can you worship this, it's plastic, a stunted misfit, with a useless red hat and a demented plastic smile. It's ridiculous, and why the bloody fishing rod?' sayeth the Lord.

'I cannot come out Lord' sayeth Adam, dodging the issue.
'And why not?' sayeth the Lord.

'I haven't got a pair of Gloria Vandervalt jeans or a Brutus sweatshirt, no Adidas trainers or Reactolite Rapide sunglasses' sayeth Adam.

'Have you got a TV behind that bush?' sayeth the Lord.

I'M TALKING TO SOMEONE ELSE'S FATHER

I was, I suppose, gay around the age of 12 and 13.

Though to be honest, glandular activity being what it is, nothing was safe around that time. I'd have attempted sexual intercourse with a tin of Swarfega if that was the only way of achieving orgasm.

It's important to declare this because there's thousands of men of all ages going round with the guilt of this development period shut away like a mutant twin, too ugly to be let into public gaze.

It is quite common for lads to become sexually aroused climbing over furniture. It is not considered incitement later in life to offer these people a chair when they visit.

SANS PRETENSION

We say 'cul de sac'
To make 'dead end' sound sunny
We say 'nouveau riche'
Instead of – working class with money

We call art 'avant garde'
When we don't understand it
Jumble sales sell 'bric a brac'
Which must be French for shit

Let's call a spud a spud
No more lies or elaborate word contortions
Chips are chips
Not pomme frites or french fries
Why say 'haute cuisine' when you mean 'smaller portions'

No more saying we had a 'tete a tete'
When you mean you've been nagging
Bragging or just chin wagging

And no more calling it a 'menage a trois'
When you mean three people shagging

WELCOME TO THE CITY OF SELF

(the above phrase was found graffitied on the Art gallery at Edinburgh during the Fringe 1990)

Welcome to the City of Self
Where the body of Christ becomes bread and jam
The beast with a thousand I's
I leaflet therefore I am

Winning boat races tie at Oxbridge
Careerists frigging in the ligging
It's the death of a sales pitch
Where the one line quote is King

Where it takes 200 to tango
Fast talking at the running buffet
Is there a medical student in the house?
Or is everyone's name really 'lovey'?

Beauty hangs it's head
Where the commonplace has no worth
Where once the touch of another hand
Might have been the greatest show on Earth

There's an old man dead in the gutter
There are razor blades stained by a bath
But in the carnival nothing else matters
Except he who gets the last laugh

Tuning up with the 'me me me'
The sell by date of the year
If Van Gogh had had to play Edinburgh
He'd have cut off his other ear

LIFE AFTER FOREVER

It's always harder for the gardener
To smell how sweet the flowers are
With the stench of manure still on his palms

From the first warm blood in the water
Nature has never invested in failure
A call for moral justice would have us all shot at dawn

There's more courage in the hand that re-enters the flame
Than all the arrogance of those yet to fail

PRAYERS FOR THE IMPERFECT

We are the imperfect
the rejected
the bruised
the damaged goods
the misshapen fruit

the crop that failed to make the grade
the eggshell that couldn't take the strain
the discounted
the allowable waste
the below standard
the bottom of the range
the potatoes with too many eyes
the slow mover putrified
the garment soiled
the bargain spoiled
the chipped and cracked
the squeezed and put back
the peas no longer tender and young
the incomplete
the thread undone
the scorned
the squashed
the marked down
the grape unwashed

We are the imperfect
the rejected
the bruised
the aborted
the discontinued

FAMOUS FOR A FIFTEENTH OF A SECOND

Forget the glass slipper of translation
Or the gay of a popular hijack

Reinventing Welsh or Dutch place names
We stumble through scriptures
No-clops to ritual languagesphere

A radiogram of lost words
The hair lacquer of techno wastage
The tin bath of nostalgia
The whip and top of naivety
The fleeting Spangles of Betamax ambition
The fantasy shortfall of the Aztec bar
The lost dreams of the twelve track cassette

The Space Hopper generation of
Smurf fashion suicide victims
No longer remember member member
What a Womble Womble Womble they were

THE UGLY DUCKLING
THAT GREW UP TO BE AN UGLY DUCK

At teenage disco's both the male and the female of the species would travel in pairs.

These would generally be termed the Goodlooking one and the Uglybastard.

A standard ploy of the Goodlooking one to create cohesion would be to say,
'It's so difficult to find a partner because there's usually a
Goodlooking one and an Uglybastard, and we're both goodlooking'.

This the Uglybastard would tend to believe
Being both ugly and stupid
and because, of course,
deep down they wanted to believe it, whether true or not.

In fact sometimes the Uglybastard would actually think that
they were indeed the Goodlooking one and feel sorry for the other
poor schmuck not realising that the only reason the Goodlooking
one was pal-ing about with them in the first place was that
they were no competition.

At this point the Uglybastard would say,
'It's so difficult to find a partner because there's usually a
Goodlooking one and an Uglybastard, and we're both goodlooking'.

The only exception to this rule is when both are Uglybastards.
(Although to create a bond the exact same wording would again be used)

THE PARTY TO WHICH YOU WERE NOT INVITED

'. . . was like no other party before.
What a party.
What a party.
Everyone was there.
Well, everyone, that is, but you.
It was incredible.
Amazing.
You wouldn't believe what went on.
I mean let's face it if you weren't at that party
then you don't know what PARTY means.
What a party.
You just couldn't imagine a party like that.
There'll never be a party like it again.
Everyone's still talking about it.
Well, everyone, that is, but you.
A party like that can change your life.
I mean any other party
is going to seem drab now in comparison.
I mean, I've been to parties with a capital P
but this was a party with a capital P A R T Y
know what I mean ?
No, I don't suppose you do.
What a party.
A party like that comes once in a lifetime, maybe.
Still at least everyone can share the memory
well, everyone, that is, . . .'

TO HELENA AND BACK

There is no reasoning to your loneliness
You build your fireside on the most barren of landscapes
You offer your resignation from the vital

You are too concerned with structure and process

Those that wallow in reminiscence
suffocating all bitterness in nostalgia
deny the pain that the body needs
to summon the adrenaline
to heal the wound

but such observation is cerebral
even the sound of the vowels is the betrayal of compassion
It's actions not words that provide the most vivid memory

The gift I would bring to your christening
is courage in all things
Let the optimism you wear shame all contrived fashion

Unholy in the church of perfection
the stairs to forgiveness
are worn with the footsteps of those that falter

And you hold up your arms to the world
You wear desperation like a weight around your shoulders

There is no reason why I should save you

There is no reason why you should save me

IS THERE NO ROOM FOR MIRACLES ALONG THE BURY ROAD?

She has an Oscar

It is a small figure
standing upright
with arms wrapped
in front of its heart
clasping a sword

It is too small to be mistaken for a shrine

It is not a real Oscar, obviously
Merely a facsimile

From the stage though
it looks just like the real thing

It's not as heavy of course
so there is an element of pretence
needed to carry off the deception

This is called acting
and is the reason she was given the honour
in the first place

It is hollow
but there is no way moisture
could have fallen from its cheeks

THE MAN WHO THOUGHT CRAIG RAINE WAS RESPONSIBLE FOR THE DEPLETION OF SCANDINAVIAN FORESTS

I discovered poetry late on
For years
I thought 'Bathos' and 'Pathos'
Were 2 of the 3 Musketeers

I thought a 'couplet'
Was a small couple
And that 'Larkin' was what Kids did
That got them into trouble

I called 'Yeats' an old boozer
But I meant no insult
'Paradise Lost' I used t'
Think was a football result

It seems such a dumb thing
And hard now to believe
'Ogden Nash' I once thought something
That Hilda did with her teeth

I thought 'Shelley' was the type of beach
Where you took your buckets and spades
And that 'Omah Kayam'
Was the man
Who bought out Remmington Blades

THE DREAM OF THE ROOD

amid 60 million pieces of heaven

some shapes appear so similar
but with 30 million two piece jigsaws
it's not the easiest of puzzles

worn and scuffed at the edges
the desperate and the unloved
force another faulty fit
hammering compromise into loose connections
distorting the surface to hide the ruptures beneath

> and always it seems the saddest feint
> the cowards selfish taunt at fate
> replacing love and hate with fixture
> painting over
> a mismatching picture

SOMEWHERE BETWEEN INTEREST AND INDULGENCE

1. There's so much trouble in the world.
   The Arabs against the Jews
   the Catholics against the Protestants
   WORLD FAMINE, EARTHQUAKE, POVERTY
   and to top it all
   I've got a cold sore.

2. OK so if all these things that happen are in God's plan
   if it's all part of a great tapestry of human experience
   how does my cold sore fit into all this?

3. We all have our crosses to bear only
   I notice Jesus never had a cold sore.

4. Perspective ? How can I get things in perspective when I've got a gigantic cold sore obscuring my view ?

5. Over-reacting, that's easy for you to say, you don't have to wake up with a huge monstrosity threatening to obliterate your entire face. It's all too much, I can't stand it any longer, I just can't stand it any longer.

6. Yes fine. It just burned itself out. Fickle, no it's not a question of fickle. By the way I see Argentina has invaded the Falklands. It was some time ago. I know that. I've been busy, I do have problems of my own you know.

IS THE UNIVERSE GOD'S BACHELOR PAD?

The heavens on high
make the tallest men shrink
all pettiness misplaced
as we cower beneath

But what if the sky
is just God's bathroom sink
the stars; blobs of toothpaste
from brushing his teeth

WAS MAN AN AFTERTHOUGHT?

Six days the making of Heaven and Earth
But with the weekend coming up soon
Not even God does his best work
On a Saturday afternoon

NEVER PLAY CHESS WITH AN ANARCHO-NIHILIST

I tried to play chess with an Anarcho-Nihilist once
Every move I made – he questioned.

He continually changed the rules
But later claimed that there weren't really any in the first place.

He said 'Any piece can go to any position on the board it wants, when it wants'.

He kept making three or four moves at a time. Then, when it suited him, he moved
my pieces out of the way. Sometimes into other rooms.

He refused to place any of the pieces centrally in the proper squares. He declared
such divisions to be 'False Borders' and started painting out the white squares at
random.

When I announced it was check mate and that I'd won
He just kicked the table over and
Flushed my King down the loo.

VICTIMS OF WAR

'VICTIMS OF WAR' building week by week into a sickening reminder of the inhuman slaughter conveniently overlooked by glossy colour magazines for war enthusiasts.

At last after 40 years of sweeping the shame under the carpet 'VICTIMS OF WAR' brings you full page photographs of sinews and bones blown from a child's naked corpse.

Marvel at authentic maps of mass murder illustrated in colour with diagrams depicting the distasteful side of war, the deformity of war veterans, the deaths through disease and decay, the mutilated bodies caught strewn across bomb-sites before being laid neatly in rows, grassed over and decorated with clean white head stones that never show the blood.

Follow train load by train load the hell of the holocaust in all its ugly fascination.

Collect the close-up pictures of concentration camps not quite cleansed of the stench of death before the first train load of American tourists.

Read personal eye witness accounts of the pain and the grief, recapture the pitiful degrading of humanity. 'VICTIMS OF WAR' available at little cost. Buy World War 1, get World War 2 free.

TABOO

(A small beauty spot on the cheek bone is considered chic
Two inches to the side and the same mark
parked on the end of the nose is seen as a personal failing)

Our deepest fears are cloistered
by what we politely term
Taboo

Death, Loneliness, Physical and Mental Disability
Disease, Old Age, The Eccentricities of our Bodies
Sexual Inadequacy

These we see as human failings
as embarassing imperfection, as grotesque lacking

It is the fear of being exposed as failure
that frightens us most
The fear that the extent of our imperfection will not be looked
upon as acceptable

It is, however, these imperfections and the universal need for
acceptance, understanding and forgiveness that distinguishes
that which we term love
The comforting of another and the submission of humour is,
perhaps our bravest victory

MID WALES CRISIS

My heart reminisces of a faster pace
like this seaside town in winter
but time and tide wait for no man
nor does the Aberystwyth sprinter.

MIDDLE AGE SPREAD

The eternal quest is but hassle
when in the test of youth
                you can no longer compete
5 minutes on a bouncy castle
and 5 days smelling of deep heat

FLUX COULD KILL

The grass leans outward
The cliff
jagged with purpose
penetrates the waves

2 feet from certain death
2 feet of existence
not menacing but matter of fact
The choice is always as narrow as this
Only here
you can measure spirit

2 feet of lies and soft options
2 feet of fear and pulse
There is a truth that's too easy to forget until you fill your
lungs with determination

At times such as dusk
there is wonder in the commonplace

Rain hangs on the skyline

Beauty is always this short a distance

I have spent my whole life trying to enter the gates of Heaven
using my heart as a battering ram

2 feet of the attainable
2 feet from acceptance

THERE WILL COME A TIME YOU WILL NO LONGER
SET ASIDE ONE DAY A WEEK FOR TEARS

your heart seems hesitant between each beat

and serenity is never so easily charted
not even on the most detailed atlas

. . . for there appears an honesty
within your quiet breathing
to which
these sad poems aspire

it is time, perhaps
to set aside a little compassion
and to court yourself

THE BLACK HOLE THAT WAS PHILLIP MITCHELL

Phillip Mitchell had been depressed for some time – aeons in fact. But it came as somewhat of a surprise to both astronomers and to his mother alike when, during a solar eclipse, Phillip Mitchell imploded.

His mother thought nothing of it at first, Phillip was always seeking attention and she felt this was just another of his little tricks. 'The universe doesn't revolve around you Phillip', she would often remark.

Even when cutlery started to go missing she refused to accept that her own son was any different from every other crazy mixed-up teenager. 'It's something he'll grow out of', she told Patrick Moore on a 'Sky at Night' special.

Not until the back bedroom and most of the upstairs landing had mysteriously disappeared did Mrs Mitchell concede that Phillip needed guidance.

Several doctors were consulted but all were sucked into the abyss, as was the remainder of the house, the top soil of the back garden and Mr Pollock's garage.

Specialists were called in but the problem was now out of hand.
Most of Greater Manchester had already vanished.

Scientists worked around the clock. All military forces were mobilised. Panic gripped the Earth.

Within days the whole of the Northern Hemisphere was no more.
In less than a week all traces of the Earth had disappeared.
The Moon quickly followed, as did the other planets in the solar system and even the Sun itself.

One by one the stars in the Milky Way were devoured until, eventually, galaxies from the furthest reaches were dragged inward.

Soon the entire universe was void.

'That'll teach them', said Phillip, sucking in the nothingness.

SUBJECTIVE OBJECTIVITY

There is wry truth
I term
Reality
Selected truth
That serves me well

But were I ruthless
With such vanity
The neglected truth
Then I
Should tell

MIME DOESN'T PAY

Last night I was burgled by a mime artist. He never made a sound. He could have got away with it, but then he tried to steal a piano I haven't got.

He pushed and he pulled, he strained and he heaved, but it wouldn't move. Maybe he thought there was something valuable behind it. There wasn't. He tried to float the piano. He blew up a balloon and tied it to the piano, then he couldn't lift the balloon.

I found him in the morning trapped inside an imaginary box. I called the police. He started to panic. He tried climbing up a fictitious ladder. When the police arrived they let him out. He made a dash for it . . . tried running away on the spot.

It took the police four hours to get him into the car, he kept getting pulled back by an invisible rope. I decided not to press charges. This afternoon, I put in an insurance claim for the piano.

MY SON THE POET

Christopher Marlowe wrote for a living
But before his name was made
What did his family make of it all
Cobblers being their trade

Blake's pop ran a hosiery shop
Burns' pop kept a vegetable crop
None of the great bards ever had
A great poet for a dad

Milton's old man was a scrivener
Making whatever scriveners make
Hardy's father was a mason
But without the funny handshake

The Chaucer clan were in wine
Not of some long literary line
Great poets it can be said
May be born but never bred

Donne's dad was an ironmonger
Shakespear senior made gloves
Keats dad shovelled horse shit
Whilst his son wrote of inner loves

THE HUMAN MEAT

Rubbing the monkey into her face
She felt more attractive already
The heart of a rabbit she used
To highlight her cheekbones
Assorted rodents she smoothed to her lips
Woodlice, cockroaches and other insects
Darkened her lashes
Whilst the blinded eyes of labradors
She dabbed behind her ears
For the final touch
She slipped into a full length mink
Turning to leave she
Caught sight of her
Reflection and squealed
With excitement
Tonight she was dressed to kill

PURITY OF SPIRIT COMES IN ALL WAIST SIZES

Patronised as character
The problem is not glandular
The problem is only the perception of glamour
A perfect anatomy provides no real armour

There is no correlation between girth and worth
We play the glands we're dealt at birth

Lift up your chins
Live fat die full
Build your bonfires on the highest of hills

Physical presence is but a folly
Only the depth of the soul is measured as holy

Angels are never spotty, hunchback, nor bald

Even heavy bone structure
Is transparent
In
The weighing of souls

THE CHOCOLATE TIN SOLDIER

Here I stand flaunting my age as a statistic
reciting my credits
on the tips of my toes
helpless

We are all creatures of our own imagination
Victims of past decisions and their consequences

I have become famous having nothing better to do whilst waiting
to fall in love
My dad always said, 'It doesn't matter what you do, so long as you do your best'

but what if your best is not enough?

Against all Gods and fate there has got to be some reason to
even the poorest of souls

As moments fall like droplets
            selfish for you
            proud; by the longest possible route
            but scared
            disturbed by your every movement
here I stand
            embarrassed like the moon at midday
This is where I fight or die
at the foothills of your humanity
helpless

SELLING THE SIZZLE AND NOT THE BACON
BUYING THE SIZZLE AND NOT THE BACON

With the electric bill pasted to the side of your face you wait and waste the Monday to Friday. Religious on payday you pray to the Gods of Gas and Rates that they don't vent their wrath as you plan your way through the Christmas / the Easter / the Summer Holidays/ mortgaging your present / keeping several bills in the air / avoiding go to jail / never passing go / never collecting two hundred / the dice aren't loaded / there's no need / Mayfair and Park Lane have already been bought / look to the chance / there's always the chance / fill in your coupon / post your coupon / and pray to the benevolent Gods Vernons and Littlewoods.

CONFESSIONS OF A CLOSET CELIBATE

Now lust can rust 'cos I'm bored of sex
My libido's just a place where dust collects

You know the first signs of tedium are on there way
When you actually start snoring during foreplay

Then you can bemoan your hormones as really down the pan
When each orgasm seems like a predictable rhyme that takes too
Long to attain, and doesn't quite scan

Once a drug upon which I thrived

Now the insertion of protruding bits of the anatomy into the
Anatomy of another to effect a momentary sensation of pleasure
Together with a short period of wellbeing all seems somewhat
Too contrived

Where once during sex
To prolong the climax
I would go through the names of all the teams in the first
Division and mentally record them

Now I do the same with the second and third
Purely to prevent boredom

POETRY AND TRAIN SPOTTING – A NATURAL AFFINITY

I saw the 'Sir John Betjeman' today
         On Piccadilly station
And I couldn't refuse
The urge to muse
Whilst I stood there contemplating
As emblazoned for posterity across a 125
His name now pulls more people
Than when he was alive

WAITING FOR LOCO

My love,
her beauty never pales
for her I'll wait
         forever

My love
she comes by British Rail
so better late
         than never

DOPEY AND JULIET

We are watching a new adaptation of Romeo and Juliet but
it is ridiculous to empathise with the leading characters

Mawkish fascination has laid waste to my valour
and my body creaks like a faulty windscreen wiper

I can no longer read the nakedness of your face
How I react is no reflection on you
How you react
is not necessarily
a reflection on me
Your eyes remain unchanged but
you wear the years apart like a new fashion

I'm sure the main actors mock my tentative appearance in this
scene
I would feel easier if this were Beauty and the Beast
or more comfortable even with the part of Dopey in Snow White

You touch my hand and reassure me that we can be friends now
I'm certain
in your version
I'm not even in this play
I have taken on the role of an old work colleague that it's
nice to see for two minutes but could become tiresome over the
course of a few drinks

LOVE POEM TO THE REVIEWERS

I wish upon you a pox
Spuds in your favourite socks
I hope you die
With the LP of your life
Marked down in the cheapie box

May you rot and burn in Hell
May you choke on your own pissy smell
May the fluff in your navel
Drive you unstable
And may you suffer verrucas as well

May all your conkers be oners
May your love life fail with dishonours
May your victories be small
And your enemies be tall
All driving thirty two tonners

May your bathwater always run cold
May your road maps never refold
May you lose all your diaries
And may Directory Enquiries
Keep you on permanent hold

SELF MUTILATION IS NO BASIS FOR A SOUND RELATIONSHIP

My ankles are blistered
The nerves raw when I try to peel back
my sock, matted with blood and shreds of skin.

I wore new shoes to the party.
I've been to too many parties since puberty
and always, it seems, in new shoes.
No matter how much they hurt
I thought
'people always look good in new shoes'.
At one point I even tried to dance but that was a mistake.
Only walking home did the pain start to cripple.

(. . . Napoleon's retreat from Moscow yet again.)

I bought plasters today but they are too small
the sticky portion would pull an open wound.

I can't even wear old comfy shoes now
and can no longer lay back on my bed.

I'm barefooted and confined to the house.

Not since childhood, I suppose, have I spent a whole day barefoot.

I'm sure it lessens the stabbing and helps the process of recovery.

Now my only concern is gangrene. Would it be considered romantic to die from
gangrene at the back of the ankles?

A TRIBUTE TO MICHAEL CLARKE

I love the grace and poise of his dance
the integrity of his artistic stance
the sheer delight
of beholding the sight
of his arse hanging out of his pants

A TRIBUTE TO L. S. LOWRY

The painting of L. S. Lowry
could not be considered flowery
but then Salford city
is not very pretty
and more often that not it's showery

A TRIBUTE TO ANDY WARHOL'S WIG

Andy Warhol was no mug
of this it can be said
he pulled the rug from under the Arts
and wore it on his head

MARKETING OF THE SOUL PLC AND OTHER INSIDER DEALINGS

Stale air
is an insult to the gift of breath

the bite of life is an exquisite step

There is no colour, fragrance or shape
to love, though bittersweet is the taste of love

There is no season for lukewarm
closeted from fields of white
numb
to the nuances of nature
and the bones of trees laced with ice

There are flowers that wilt in constant summer
There is a despair
                    that kills more than the bleakest winter
Loud wallpaper
will never replace a lovers murmur

If only the saints would give birth
If only the smallest dreams came true
Maybe some night
when street lights enrapture the stars
and Heaven
comes down
to kiss the roofs

A belief in magic is no lack of respect
To wish
is but to brave the spirits furthest edge

THE POEM WITH NO NAME

In the movie
he rode away into the sunset.
But the next day
I saw him shopping
in Tesco. Some check-out
woman gave him a bad time
and he never even shot
her once. Which only
goes to prove Tesco
isn't like real life at all.

SOUTHERN CEMETERY – THE CLASS OF 92

Like comic timing
Old graves
Bedded well in hard ground
Sit easy in glib abstract

With assurance of place
Haircuts grown out
Mourners long since rejoined
Our great grandfathers surrender their individuality

In the grandeur of their anonymity
We grieve more for humanity than our own mortality

Then we come upon God's latest crop
Fresh mounds of loose soil
Soft like a hand on your brow
A scar still pink before the skin hardens

There's something disturbing
About the grouping of these
Well tended plots at the edge of the gate

The unweathered granite
The unworn epitaphs
Like first year kids in their new uniforms
As rich and brown as a new satchel

Anxious like their mother
We hesitate at the railings
'Take care of Uncle John'
'Take care of her'

On the far side of the high street
There's a choice of undertakers
And a discreet distance down the road you can buy flowers

SELF IMAGE BEING AT THE CORE OF MOTIVATION

She never had a full length mirror of her own.
As a child
she played make believe
in front of her mother's dresser.

But now in her bedsit
all she has is a small bathroom unit set into the wall.
The light is not flattering
and she is never drawn to check her reflection.
Her new dresses
she never sees in full glory.
It's no wonder she shies to the corners, arms crossed in front
and head lowered.

Occasionally in the midst of distraction
when out shopping
she will catch her reflection in a shop window.
Occasionally
she'll linger those extra seconds to think she could compete.
Of course
she knows the glass is dark
and there is an element of distortion.

She will probably never
have the confidence to buy herself a proper mirror.

AFTER ALL THE RAIN THAT'S FALLEN

I have decided to re-paint my rainbow
It's been a little neglected lately
Some of the colours have grown faint

I've been meaning to
touch up the worst of the bits worn thin
but rainbows are always so high
and my step ladders can't reach

It's in the nature of rainbows, so I've
always been told,
that at some point they touch the Earth
and
now that I've found where this is
I'll be
round to your house Sunday
to make an early start

If you can,
could you move that pot of yellow
out of the way, my love ?

You have never seen a colour so bright
as the colours I shall bring for you.

TURNING STRAIGHT TO THE SPORTS PAGES

The shoes worn by clowns are always too big
Real giants are rare amid
The side shows of cowardice and guilt
The vain deception of dwarfs on stilts

Even
The gravestones of the famous eventually Rot
The ashes of the tallest men
Won't fill a small piss pot

Those passed have long outnumbered those bound
Every house is built on a cemetery
The Earth is all burial ground
Washed by the souls of those lost at sea

And when God and Science has reckoned
In less
Than a millionth of a second
All the atoms of the universe will be crammed in
To a space smaller than the head of a pin.
There will be a huge explosion
And everything
Will start all over again

Discovering your scent in the summer rain
Redefining a puddle as a small lake

BOOKS BY HENRY NORMAL NOW IN PRINT –

From:

> A..K. DISTRIBUTION,
> 22 LUTTON PLACE,
> EH8 9PE
> TEL:/FAX: 031 6671507

A MORE INTIMATE FAME

> A5 Book, 120 pages, glossy cover, bound.
> Price £6.60 (inc. p&p).

THE DREAM TICKET (Second Edition)

> A5 Booklet, 52 pages, glossy cover, bound.
> Price £5.40 (inc. p&p).

THE FIFTEENTH OF FEBRUARY (Second Edition)

> A5 Booklet, 52 pages, glossy cover, bound.
> Price £5.40 (inc. p&p).

THE THIRD PERSON

> A5 Booklet, 56 pages, glossy cover, bound.
> Price £5.40 (inc. p&p).

Some Recent Titles from AK Press

ECSTATIC INCISIONS: THE COLLAGES OF FREDDIE BAER by Freddie Baer, preface by Peter Lamborn Wilson; ISBN 1 873176 60 0; 80 pages, a three color cover, perfect bound 8 1/2 x 11; £7.95. This is Freddie Baer's first collection of collage work; over the last decade her illustrations have appeared on numerous magazine covers, posters, t-shirts, and album sleeves. Includes collaborations with Hakim Bey, T. Fulano, Jason Keehn, and David Watson.

SOME RECENT ATTACKS: ESSAYS CULTURAL AND POLITICAL - by James Kelman; ISBN 1 873176 80 5; 96pp; £4.50. In this collection, Kelman directs his linguistic craftsmanship and scathing humor at targets ranging from "private profit and public loss" to the "endemic racism, class bias and general elitism at the English end of the Anglo-American literary tradition."

INNA LIVERPOOL - by Benjamin Zephaniah; ISBN 1 873176 75 9; 24pp; £1.95. A selection of poems representing a small portion of Zephaniah's work as Poet/Writer in Residence with the Africa Arts Collective in 1988/89.

ON THE MASS BOMBING OF IRAQ AND KUWAIT, COMMONLY KNOWN AS THE "GULF WAR" - by Tom Leonard; ISBN 1 873176252; 24pp; £1.95. Written as the 'allies' perpetrated the mass execution of the Iraqi people, On the Mass Bombing ... exposes the hypocrisy and deceit of politicians and the military, and the media's complicity, in a concerted attempt at the wholesale destruction of a country, its people and infrastructure.

THE ASSAULT ON CULTURE: UTOPIAN CURRENTS FROM LETTRISME TO CLASS WAR - by Stewart Home; ISBN 1 873176 30 9; 128pp two color cover perfect bound 5 1/2 x 8 1/2; £5.95. "A straightforward account of the vanguards that followed Surrealism: Fluxus, Lettrisme, Neoism, and other even more obscure." *Village Voice.*

AK Press publishes, distributes to the trade, and retails mail order a wide variety of radical literature. For our latest catalog featuring these and several thousand other titles, please send a large self-addressed, stamped envelope to:

AK Press	AK Press
22 Lutton Place	P.O. Box 40682
Edinburgh, Scotland	San Francisco, CA
EH8 9PE, Great Britain	94140-0682 U.S.A.